BOA
EDITIONS
LIMITED

The Vandals

Poems by

ALAN MICHAEL PARKER

BOA Editions, Ltd.   ❋   Rochester, NY   ❋   1999

LC #: 98–76203
ISBN: 978–1–880238–74–5

07 08 09 4 3 2

Publications by BOA Editions, Ltd.—
a not-for-profit corporation under section 501 (c) (3)
of the United States Internal Revenue Code—
are made possible with the assistance of grants from
the Literature Program of the New York State Council on the Arts,
the Literature Program of the National Endowment for the Arts,
the Lannan Foundation, the Sonia Raiziss Giop Charitable Foundation,
the Eric Mathieu King Fund of The Academy of American Poets,
as well as from the Mary S. Mulligan Charitable Trust,
the County of Monroe, NY,
and from many individual supporters.

Cover Design: Daphne Poulin-Stofer
Typesetting: Richard Foerster
BOA Logo: Mirko

BOA Editions, Ltd.
Nora A. Jones, Executive Director/Publisher
Thom Ward, Editor/Production
Peter Conners, Editor/Marketing
Glenn William, BOA Board Chair
A. Poulin, Jr., President & Founder (1938 - 1996)
250 North Goodman Street, Suite 306
Rochester, NY 14607
www.boaeditions.org

for Felicia and Eli

CONTENTS

※

The Vandals

THE VANDALS

In the poem about the vandals, the vandals
Back their Dodge 4 x 4 up to the door

Of the abandoned town hall and theater.
In untied boots, they carry canvas bags

And carry off the oak wainscoting.
Above the wings and pit and stage, the ghosts

Of two starved porcupines command
Twin mounds of scat, respectively,

The prickly hats of king and fool.
(The chairs don't care, bottoms up, attentive.)

As the vandals stomp inoutinoutinoutinout
All in one breath because poetry

Is an oral tradition, the ghosts of the porcupines
Fill the air with rhyme: Visigoths and mishegas,

Gerkin and curtain, howitzers and trousers.
The vandals stomp inoutinoutinoutinout:

In their arms the split and pocked wood,
In their wake the porcupines

Are unaware of God's universal love.
In the poem, no one is free:

The ghosts of the two porcupines
Got in but they can't get out,

Starving over and over. The vandals—
Who sometimes look like you

And sometimes me—will never
Go home to cozy vandal homes

To make of their deeds a poem.
In the poem about the vandals,

Because a poem is an abandoned theater,
The porcupines have eaten the scenery:

Padua, Venice, Alexandria, Verona, gone;
Love prostrate on its pyramid.

And the vandals stomp inoutinoutinoutinout,
And the vandals stomp inoutinoutinoutinout.

ANOTHER POEM ABOUT THE VANDALS

In another poem about the vandals, the vandals
Toss their dullèd knives

Onto a table, scattering three hours' worth
Of peanut shells. A chant goes up:

More beer, more beer, more beer.
A barmaid waves, stubs out her cigarette—

Vaguely aware of waiting to die,
Restless in the blue TV light.

Separate checks, the vandals roar
In unison, as though they weren't

In a poem. The barmaid
Adjusts her bra, thinks about

How pretty
Abstract Expressionism makes sorrow seem.

Where is that bitch? the vandals roar,
Just as the inexorable force of

History pushes her out into the snow:
More beer, more beer, more beer.

She has to try to quit the poem, and the vandals.
She closes the back door, glances toward

You and me—did she see us?—
And turns her collar up against the night.

BEFORE THE VANDALS

In the poem about the vandals
Who have yet to arrive, you and I

Are lovers, our caresses no less
Sad or urgent for what will be.

The vandals have been sighted
Near the city walls, as close

As they will get, because the words
Of a poem only represent the real.

The vandals sing their raucous songs
Around their cookfires smoking in the rain,

Vulgar songs heard far away:
You trace the line of my jaw with your

Wet finger, smile, grind
A bit against my groin, smear me

With your blowzy mouth, your tongue.
(My blowzy mouth. Yours.)

In the poem our room fills
With the acrid stink of rabbit stew,

The future ends with a declarative sentence,
And no one can hear the dead

Save the living. We know, you and I,
That somewhere beyond the walls

The vandals stir their vandal stews
And reminisce of gingerbread men.

We know the vandals have their own ideas
About what they'll do with me, with you.

BETWEEN POEMS THE VANDALS GO

Behind the iron bleachers,
Playing football in the snow.

Blue jeans black as bruises, stiff with ice,
The vandals clap their hands,

Shuffle frozen toes in beat up hightops
And two pairs of woolly socks.

They pretend to be
Greek heroes, charging into violence

Like tired lovers, relentless as a poem.
They pretend they're you and me.

On the other side of the bleachers,
The real game continues: the marching band

Cuts up the artificial turf, the tuba and the drums
Warm the hearts of boys and girls.

Cheers festoon the air—
Then helmets crack, a whistle blows,

The vandals shake their heads,
Pack up their liniments and cardigans,

And trudge on off, beyond
The parking lot

To where the little yellow buses
Idle odorously in lines.

Dumb words, the vandals mutter,
Squeezing through and squeezing by.

WITHOUT THE VANDALS

In this poem there are no vandals;
There is no history, no pin-pricked map

Spread across the stainèd cot, no tracer fire
Reflected in the aide-de-camp's pince nez.

Where are the vandals? we ask
Ourselves aloud. Where can they be?

Words arrive from the front,
Secreted in letters, sewn into the lining

Of a courier's wool overcoat.
He is exhausted, he needs a room;

He hammers on the bell at the front desk
Of a roadside motel, where a sleepy clerk

Compares signatures to license plates,
The ol' monotony of love.

Because a poem writes its own rules,
We can only hope the night will end,

As all nights do, any minute, soon.
In the motel's little office, an oldish dog

Scratches flat her cedar bed, settles down.
A computer hums like God, hum, hum.

If only the vandals would kick in the door,
Try to tear your hand from mine,

(Through the galleria, last room on the left.)
The TV speaks in tongues;

A neon sign flashes through the drapes,
NO VACANCY, NO VACANCY,

NO VACANCY, NO VACANCY,
A dialectic lullaby.

(In the darkness of the poem
We whisper to each other soothingly.)

VANDALS, HORSES

The vandals are dreaming, wolves are dreaming,
The horses are staked to their deaths.

In the poem of the vandals dreaming
A word bites through a lip,

Drawing blood. (The poem is in ruins.)
The vandals dream their arms unseen,

Dream themselves buried in the belly
Of the birthing mare, as a foal is

Torn to life. (The poem is banal
As the barn is bloody.)

And you and I, and you and I, we steal
Each other's blankets, wrap ourselves

In darkness, wind, in anything
The night will let us, to feel safe.

Do you feel safe? (Soft,
The vandals sleep.) Because a word

Is a dream of its meaning, you and I
Must dream the vandals dreaming:

Soft, the horses nicker in the barn.
(Soft, our poem begins as vandals dream.)

PHILOSOPHY, THE VANDALS SAY

Is no better than a poem. There they lie,
Those vandals, drinking before noon;

They have come to build the neighbor's
Cedar deck one Saturday, beer after beer:

She loves me, she loves me not.
The vandals glow in safety-orange

Hunters' garb and camouflage, they glow
Like words highlighted on a page.

Near the trees, a deer leaps into
The future, a flash of the letter A:

The vandals stare, betwixt, agog;
The cedar deck remains unbuilt

Within its beams, neither Being nor Becoming.
In our house next door, a picture window

Pictures nothing; we lie untouching,
Spent, neither Being nor Becoming,

Side by side. Philosophy, the vandals say,
And then their words trail off like . . .

The vandals know they're safe,
In the nation of their making;

They slap each other's back, pretend
That comedy is love. And you and I?

We prop ourselves with pillows, watch
The watchful deer nibble on a peony

—Are we kept within her gaze?—
Until she leaps into the greenery:

Gone, inscrutable, that blur beyond
The legible, within the trees' mad alphabet.

＊

ABANDONING ALL PRETENSE, THE VANDALS

Occupy the poem. They stake
Fluorescent tents around the public fountain,

Pan the water for our wishes,
Whistle in the literal night at all

The pretty boys and girls. In the morning,
After eggs and scrapple, 'round

The rugged rocks the vandals run,
Snapping towels, trampling the daffodils

The Ladies' Club had planted with their monogrammèd
Garden gloves. Then down the street

Through every town, poem after poem
In pairs the vandals rage—through the vacant

Snack bars and roller rinks, the Putt-Putts
And deserted Drive-Ins of the ordinary heart.

Where are you? they shout. Come out
And play! Don't you want to play?

(What with time left on the meter,
Clothes frying in the dryer, a chicken

Chickening in every pot . . .) We see you there,
The vandals call. Come join the fun!

(What with bombs going off in letters,
What with packing up the future . . .)

Abandoning all hope, the vandals
Leave the poem to us, to our devices.

And you and I? We curl into our lives
Of least resistance, giggle underneath

The blankets, play a game called
Catch the vandal if you can.

*

THE VANDALS AND THE MOON

They have been waiting, these vandals,
For someone to come and rescue them;

They are O, so tired of meaning.
In a clearing in the woods

They have built a fort of mud and sticks
And a barbecue pit for the roasting of meat,

For the joy of *jus* sticky in the beard.
There the vandals clog and jig

In the light of the roseate moon, the moon
(Writing its only line

Over, over,
Across the sky.)

Because they are the vandals,
They would eat each other, yum.

They would fix a liquid gaze
On you, on me, on you again,

Pure in their class consciousness
As the rich inevitably become.

(If only they saw us hiding there,
Pine needles needling our sweaters;

Twigs and leaves, the words we use
Our tinny, empty tunes.) Where are

The party favors? the vandals growl
All in one breath because

Terror is the art of restraint.
What are the bugles blowin' for?

(And the roseate moon secedes,
Nails itself to a tree;

And the moon, the moon
Tangles itself in your hair.)

※

PRACTICING THEIR DIFFIDENCE, THE VANDALS

Fill their bodies with their ghosts
The way a poem fills itself with words.

It's yet another Sunday, church-rush brunch,
Everyone festooned, all the vandals

In their wingtips, boaters, and seersucker suits
Tapping ashes from their Cuban cheroots

Into the rubber trees and potted ferns, all the ferns
Burgeoning despite the blinding light

Of art. The vandals are out
To eat again, yoo-hoo-yoo-hoo-yoo-hoo!

They wave Italian breadsticks in the air,
Spin tiny tropical umbrellas seized

From complimentary Mai Tais. Looks like
A lousy musical, mutters the assistant chef,

As he peeks through the window of the kitchen door
And wipes his favorite cleaver on a dirty rag.

I'm cooking for the chorus of "Easter Parade."
The vandals menace him with twenty orders

Of the broiled eel, hold the teriyaki;
They clutch their chests in mock arrest,

Feign heart attacks as social unrest, happy
To make a scene. He's unperturbed,

The assistant chef: he knows the vandals
Have to go, he knows which hostess peddles dope.

Water, water, everywhere, the vandals call—
And then, as if the lights had suddenly

Gone down and the audience walked out,
The vandals look around, see themselves

Grown older, see their ghosts
In every empty glass. It's only a poem,

They whisper to each other.
It's only a poem, it's only a poem, it's only a poem.

THE VANDALS DYING

In the poem about their dying
The vandals bellow for their nurses,

Slather all the smoke alarms
With Jell-O, rip every goddamned

Tube from every goddamned arm.
Where's the sawbones? they holler.

Bring on the leeches and the MRI!
A candystriper, just fifteen, beleaguered

In her future body, colors in each "O"
In *Cosmopolitan*. She knows already

That the dying never die by yelling.
Deal, the vandals roar, enthralled;

Two hearts, the bidding opens.
Because a poem can do no more

Than deny its expectations,
The candystriper dozes, dreams

The Scream by Edvard Munch, colors in
The mouth. In their semiprivate rage,

The vandals play and play,
Each gesture vaguely ceding to its ghost.

The candystriper wakes, bleary
—Where am I?—at the nurses' station,

Her candystripèd cuff
Soaking up a cup of soup,

The callboard lit before her,
Buzzing, blinking, calling

Someone, anyone, even God above,
Who's busy in another poem, busy dying.

ONLY VANDALS

In the poem with only vandals in the poem,
The vandals rev the engine of their 4 x 4,

Idle roughly at the light, smush their faces
On the glass. They are proud

At last to be the parody they wannabe.
There ain't no cops, they shout.

We have you now! The vandals
Play the brake, jounce the truck

To rock-and-roll, fill the cab with smoke,
Take hands and sing their saddest

Vandal songs of nights beyond the poem.
(The moon floats by, irreducible.)

Catty-corner to the corner store,
A strip mall bares its emptiness:

Quik Fill, Food Town, Meat Land and
A Bar-'N-Grill no more than signs,

Meaning without life. The vandals
Rifle through their lunch bags,

Rummage underneath the seats, turn
Their pockets inside out, palms upraised,

Uneasy not to have . . .
In the poem because a poem

Is only an approximation,
The vandals live the life they only

Can imagine. (And they are the vandals,
And they can't imagine more than . . .)

And the lights begin to change
As all lights do, any moment, soon,

This to that, to this.
And the vandals rev the engine

Of whatever, and the vandals
Smush their faces on the glass.

*

IN THE WRONG POEM THE VANDALS

Find themselves adrift, their souls
Like paper lanterns on a still pond.

It's night. 1:30ish.
The thirsty animals have come

To slake their thirsty thirsts,
Bereft of irony: one porcupine

Eyes another skeptically,
Neo-Platonist to Manichean,

Each to each. It's all wrong,
The vandals mutter. We need to . . .

A hippo opens wide, auditioning the darkness;
A pair of white-naped cranes

Performs an icky two-step,
Shaking gobs

Of mud
From dainty feet.

Meanwhile, alone, violating
The vandals' empty home,

You and I tiptoe needlessly. The quiet
Folds upon itself where'er we go,

(Opening their cupboards,
Guzzling their eggnog,

Rumpling their sheets.)
It's only fair, you say, halfheartedly.

A cursor blinks. A kiss.
A light goes on, stays on, on.

The vandals reel within their skulls;
The porcupines tickle one another's bellies;

And the vandals hope but will not pray.
(Another light goes on.)

And the wrong poem
Ends wrong.

WITH VENGEANCE AND DESIRE, THE VANDALS

Have us where they want. We're all
In the damnèd poem together,

In a room and a vision splendid.
The vandals flick green bits of

Something from their teeth,
Claw their itchy arms raw.

A chant goes up, a chant goes down.
Because a word can do no more

Than offer us its emptiness,
The poem is an empty room

(Save the vandals, you and me, and the
Occasional wicker chair.) Where do

You think you're going? the vandals growl.
You think you're outta here?

In the eaves, an animal—a bird? a squirrel?—
Scratches itself a nest. Underneath

The dusty floor, under there, we're sure
The soil teems with dying.

(A wicker chair creaks;
The light doesn't matter.)

Because a poem is an empty room
—Save yourself, we whisper to each other—

The vandals crack a fresh deck
Of markèd cards, flip

Poker chips across and back across
Bruised knuckles. This is you,

They sneer. Watch the fingers
Never leave the hand.

AND YOU AND I

In the poem, words hide behind their letters
Like little kids playing tag,

A'giggle in a stand of snowy pine.
Home free, they shout. You're it!

In the poem a rabbit hops by. Hop.
A teenage hunter blows off

The rabbit's head. Boom!
(Hush, you take my hand in yours.

They're only words.)
Another rabbit hops by.

Boom! Another rabbit dies.
(Touch me here, you whisper.

Here, here.) In the poem a teenage hunter
Wipes the peach juice dribbling down

His daughter's chin, thinks about
Chagall in flight over Vladivostok,

A man living as his ghost.
Boom! goes a rabbit in a puff of

Buckshot, decimated, almost beautiful.
In the poem you and I hide behind

Our words, hoping for the season
To change as the season will.

(Mm, you say. Mmmmm.)
Boom! A poem steps out

From behind its meaning. Boom!
And a rabbit hops. Hop. Hop.

Away it hops, away, hop:
White on white on snow.

Boom!
Boom!

AT THE CARWASH THE VANDALS SING

Born to be wii-iii-llld, and pretend
To smash their air guitars.

It's another Tuesday night,
Free wash and wax with every fill-up,

And the vandals have arrived
To howl with glee at the scratchless brushes,

Stuff their pockets with Bags O' Mints,
Mini chess, *Highlights* for the vandal kids

The vandals never hope
To have. Git your motor runnin'!

The vandals bellow to the Wonder-All,
The Magic Mist. Out on-on the thru-way!

With fists the vandals pound the wall,
Drum the observation glass; they stomp

To the soapy roller's thrum, free
To be the Id

A vandal aims to be. At the checkout counter,
Yellow in the washlight, a youngish woman

Counts the seconds to her next cigarette,
OneMarlboroOne, TwoMarlboroTwo,

Every fifty-nine
Another

Pencil mark, a pleasure
Principle denied. She twirls a strand of hair,

Fidgets with her nose ring, and thinks about
All those elephants Hannibal loosed

In Italy. The vandals fill her store
With need, their noise

A sexual idea. Where are
The Playboy bunnies? they holler.

Where's the beef jerky?
She has to leave the vandals

To the life she's left already,
Where danger masquerades as love.

It's history, she thinks, repeating herself
As the carwash ends—and up above

The world
The night stops.

Hey! the vandals shout.
Who cut the lights?

In the reflected glow of the Snak Paks,
She tends her little need:

Tar and ash and nicotine,
Her ghost manipulating every

Finger, every flame.
Born to be wii-iii-llld,

Sing the vandals less assuredly
As they stumble toward the EXIT—

Toward home, the poem abandoned,
As though they could go home.

THE GOD OF THE VANDALS

The god of the vandals is a vandal,
He taketh many forms.

He rhymeth and he rhymeth not:
Abraham and *traffic jam,*

Sarah and *um . . . uh . . .*
He careth not for you, for me.

In the poem of old, as the story goes,
Over the foamy brine, on wings unseen,

The god of the vandals appeared
And said to the prophets . . .

And it was good.
With sand in their hair,

Under a pin-pricked sky,
In the stink and the reek

Of turtle roasted in the shell,
The vandals wept in his presence.

(And the jellyfish wept in the waves.)
And the god of the vandals

Rhymeth *Harley Davidson* and
Born again; he rhymeth

And he rhymeth not. And he
Careth not, and it was good.

And the tears of the jellyfish
Were for you, for me.

＊

THE VANDALS AND THE LAW

In the poem about the vandals and the law,
The vandals lock the door,

Dim the office overheads, set the motion
Sensors to their most sensitive.

Comeuppance or retribution?
The vandals can't decide,

Because a poem has no consequences.
In pinstripe suits and power ties, fedoras

Cocked, their dullèd knives concealed,
(Their dullèd eyes revealing neither

Joy nor rage), the vandals pretend to be
The criminals we want them to be.

What fun! they snicker in the intercom.
Shhh and Pssst and Fffft,

They stage their whispers.
Outside the corporate entity, restless

In the parking lot, you and I tickle fancies,
Play a game called Higher Moral Reasoning.

Judge or jury? asks the spider
Of the fly. Buzz, buzz, buzz,

Say the vandals to their hidden microphones.
Test, onetwothree, test, onetwothree.

In the poem because a poem is
No more than ideology

Gussied up as art, the vandals think . . .
And the long arm of whatever

Threatens neither you nor me.
And the vandals pretend to fall asleep

Upon their organized but messy desks
In the purr of machines, machines.

VANDALS IN THE GARDEN

A riot of forsythia, a six-pack
Of bougainvillea, a giggle of pansies,

A hush of lavender. In the poem
About the vandals in the garden, the vandals

Shuffle all the words like cards:
Toad! Toad! Toad! Toad!

They shout at a cedar bench.
With-teria, they lisp

To a handful of marble stones.
The vandals scratch their heads,

Dig their steel-toed boots into the humus,
(Humus the color of dirt.)

Heart attack! the vandals yell in unison,
As though language weren't linear.

Heart attack! they castigate a worm.
(The hedges don't care, neat

As the hand of God allows.)
In the poem about the vandals

In the garden, you and I cower in a corner
Of our pre-modern bucolics,

Our little picnic dismantled by
The zigs of crazèd ants

Zagging toward their ziggurat.
The letter B! The future of my death!

(The vandals pass around the pork rinds.)
The sky's a trumpet, the wind's a sea,

O lie with me, the vandals sing.
The war is wine.

※

THE VANDALS AND THE PHILISTINES

In the poem about the vandals and the Philistines,
The vandals screech to a stop in the parking lot,

Their 4 x 4 just about aglow next to the Philistines'
El Camino. In overalls and untied boots,

Bandannas knotted into mock cravats,
The vandals muss their hair, then

Rush the tavern: inininininininin!
(Saloon-style doors

Out
Of synch, slapping

Air.) Boilermakers everywhere!
The vandals shout. A round

Of Row, Row, Row Your Boat!
In the corner, chalking cues, piling up

Their quarters, the Philistines sip
Brandy Alexanders, kick the unplugged

Jukebox like a dog. Above the bar,
Bedezined in bejewelled glass,

The ghost of a wayward owl fills the scene
With shit and feathers, flailed at by a broom.

The vandals sing Top-40,
Because a poem without

Music is only a story;
The Philistines counter with

An *a capella* medley of commercials,
The suffering of launderers,

The mortification of the stained.
In the poem, as the comedy escalates,

And the ghost of the little owl
Settles near the beernuts,

The vandals and the Philistines begin
To weep. Why are they crying?

We ask ourselves aloud.
(Third booth from the back.)

What will come of us?
And the vandals and the Philistines

Rush outoutoutoutoutout!
Into the darkness beyond the poem.

And you and I, alone, remain—
Bandaging our wedding rings

With Band-Aids, wiping
Noses on each other's sleeves.

*

IN THE ABANDONED MINE THE VANDALS

Titter in their miners' hats and coveralls,
The beams of their forehead lamps

Crossed, uncrossed, careening
O'er their ghosts. They have come

To no good, once more, these vandals—
To play a game called Underground Disaster.

(In the tunnels, bright as a canary,
Words glow exactly

As they were forsaken:
Bitumen, anthracite, cordite, TNT.)

The vandals wield their picks and shovels
For effect, test their shrillest

Whistles against the echoing unknown.
Because a poem can only be

Abandoned, the vandals fill
Their canvas bags with nothing,

Drag the bags along, pretend
To lay their burdens down.

Miles deeper: silence.
(What is this vaingloriousness?

Asks the rat of the poison cheese.)
And you and I? In our toy

Miners' hats, our coveralls, we cough
The coughs of those

Dedicated to the death. And the vandals
Clamber up the walls, sliding

Down for fun. Fun!
(And the batteries in the lights run out.)

⁜

VANDAL SEX

In the poem about vandal sex,
The vandals tarry, naked in the van,

All the vandals spreading wide
Their hands to cover up their dainties,

Massive hands the size of fig leaves.
A hookah gurgles. A velvet stag

Leaps forever into a velvet glade.
(Does someone smell of peppermint?

Could it be you? It's nice.)
In the poem because a poem

Only represents sensation,
The vandals pass each other little notes

Folded into little squares
(Above the tiger rug,

The lava lamp aglow to
Cut the glare

Of art.) A howl goes up
As a hand waves a piece of paper:

What do the arrows mean?
Is anyone here fifteen?

In the poem about vandal sex,
Sex is only a metaphor for . . .

And you and I? We peek
Through the bubbled windows,

Fog the glass with quickened breath
—Hh, hh, hh, hh—

Unbutton our top buttons,
Say a little prayer. We're next.

IN THE PRE-DAWN LIGHT WHICH IS THE POEM

The vandals have been heard from yet again:
Forming up, Ten-Hut!, a tattoo

On the foggy bayou.
Bayonets affixed, party kilts awry,

The vandals bellow in the mist,
Grope for each other's shoulders,

Blind as a soul must be
Without a body.

Near the cypress trees
At the edge of the poem,

A bear sucks salmon from a bone,
Free at last of fairy tale:

Slurp, slurp, slurrrrpp.
On the other side of the clearing,

A Girl Scout flumps upon
A splintery stump, giving up,

Her tights bestriped by runs,
And thinks about

How a society manages
To house its art but not its poor.

Let's get 'em, boys!
The vandals shout. Once more over the top!

The bear smells of bear.
The Girl Scout smells of Girl Scout,

As she levels the sights of her BB gun—
At you? At me?—oblivious to

All forms of karmic debt.
And the vandals take arms against

The fog, as they wrestle with
Their ghosts in the light of nothing

And razz the coming dawn.
And the poem ends

Too easily, as some poems do,
With the bear, the girl, me and you.

✳

WORK, THE VANDALS SAY

Has no social value. It's another
Monday afternoon, 4ish, another poem,

Another adamantine hour spent
Harassing the milliner, trying on

Each Stetson, bowler, black beret;
Tossing down the Bloody Marys from

A thermos labeled Drink.
Where's the little boy? the vandals sneer,

Brandishing their celery sticks.
Didn't you have a kid?

The milliner is careful not to glance
Back toward the beaded curtain—

Where, beyond, hiding in the stock room
A child namèd Innocence

Builds a castle out of spools.
Gimme that, the vandals pout. That's mine!

And you and I? We pretend
The poem is big enough for all,

Snap our brims down low, no strangers
To this moral indolence. Kitty Genovese!

The vandals chant. Follow orders,
Follow orders, follow orders!

And the milliner forgets
That art is merely parallel to history:

He nonchalants his way to the little store's
Little door, unplugs the Welcome Mat,

Winks at you, at me, and steps into
The murderous traffic.

Woah, the vandals snort.
'Tis a pity, the vandals agree.

GROUP PORTRAIT WITH VANDALS

In the poem about the photograph,
The vandals pose against a cardboard beach and sea,

A cardboard family spread before us
Like the future: Ambrosia salad, cribbage,

Connect-the-dots, and plaid Bermudas
On a stripèd towel. (A mother's

Terror, a father's rage, a Great Aunt's
Dentures dashed upon the sand.)

For the camera, for posterity, the vandals
Mug and preen and glower;

They deliver nougies, dead arms,
Wrap one another in half-nelsons,

Proud to be the cast of the
Photographer's memories. Who is this?

You ask, your hand inching above my knee.
(We're on the sofa, in the sexualized

Embrace of old upholstery.)
That's you, I say. That's me.

*

ON THE TURNPIKE THE VANDALS

Signal left when veering right,
Slalom in and out and in and out

And in and out, between, around
Construction safety cones, every

Hellbent swerve accompanied by
An operatic Woooo! Road-trip,

The vandals belt on cue, as though
The poem had told them to.

Houston, we have a problem,
They croon into the cigarette lighter,

Resetting the trip odometer. Up ahead
At the tolls, a nineteen-year-old

Budding stock car driver tries to read
Thus Spake Zarathustra between the

Ching, the chang, the ching-de-ching
Of capitalism. The vandals

Pull into his lane, grind their gears, stall—
Pleased to hold up traffic.

He's unperturbed; he knows how little
Time means to a teen.

(His ghost lies waiting in the back
Of his sister's bondoed '86 Camaro,

Row 2 in the HQ lot.) The vandals toss
A slug, a Loony, and three pesos

Into the conical kitty. (The poem
Slows, via punctuation.)

Out and out and out and out and
In and in and in and in, the vandals

Pull a Chinese fire drill—as the toll taker
Checks his Swatch, his new tattoo, his

Macramé friendship bracelet. And the vandals
Burn rubber in their 4 x 4, race past you and me

—We might be lucky. Are you feeling lucky?—
Toward cloverleafs and breakdown lanes,

Exit ramps and radar, signs reduced to signs.
And because they are the vandals

And a poem has no future, the vandals drive
And drive and drive and drive and drive.

UNDER THE BIG TOP THE VANDALS

Are uneasy, the poem about the circus
Not what a poem should be.

A clown sets fire to a painting of a clown,
Waves around a Clown School degree;

Upon a rhinestone throw, a poodle whines
—Eeww, eeww, eeww, eeww, eeww—

Its mouth too small to bite a vandal leg.
Sidling up to the lion cage, where lions

Line up in lovely lines,
The vandals try to strike some

Fear into each other's minds:
Here kitty, kitty, kitty.

Because a poem about a circus is already
A tragicomedy, the vandals throw themselves

Down into the sawdust,
Sawdust the color of God's good eye.

And you and I? We twirl our little
Flashlights in the darkening night,

Our cotton-candied hands
Bedevilled by what only man can make.

(The vandals gaze upon each other;
A panther eyes its meat.) Outside

The wind begins to blow:
It's wind. It blows. Blow, blow.

The Big Top ripples o'er the crowd,
A drumroll rolls, a human cannonball

Becomes the end of a sentence.
(Blow winds, blow.)

Because they are the vandals, the vandals
Imagine that the weather will . . .

And the animals in the poem
(When not performing, just another zoo)

Roar their roars and paw their paws,
Wild-eyed in the gloaming;

Resigned to pace their lives like
Words inside a poem, like me, like you.

*

VANDALS, NOISE

The vandals' Friday afternoon is full of noise:
The znnznnznn of the tablesaw,

The tcktcktck of the woodchips chipped,
The whswhswhswhs of dust. In the poem

About the vandals at the lumberyard
(Another Friday afternoon, another

Act reduced to ritual),
The vandals ripple sheets of tin,

Making thunder, shaking bags of nails
Like rain. (Like rain

Words
Spill.)

Glue, glue, glue, glue, glue!
The vandals chant, their staple guns

In holsters, their leather belts askew.
Upstairs, adding up

The Income and the Outflow,
A CPA stops work, recounts

The instant he became
Half-full with grief. (A fly

Rhymes buzz with does.)
The CPA steps to the railing of the mezzanine,

Looks down upon the vandals
In their *mis-en-scène*.

Two-by-fours, two-by-fours, two-by-fours,
The vandals roar. He smiles,

Cries. He has to try
To quit his marriage, the poem,

The nightly laugh his mother dies with
In his dreams. He climbs the railing

At the moment you and I
Walk in—My god! What will happen?

Oh my god!—lifts his foot and then . . .
The vandals shake their heads;

(A fly rhymes buzz with does,
The only rhyme it knows.)

CHANSON (OU SONT LES VANDALS?)

Pretty pretty pretty lies the day
In its banality, as *les pensées*

Repeat themselves in a simple vase.
The baby on the dhurri is neither

Sad nor happy, just a baby just like
You are you and I am me. *En le chanson*

So hoity-toity, chi-chi, whoop-de-do,
The whirligig, the roundelay, the jazz of

Sound supplant all meaning.
(But it's French and so it sounds . . .)

Sad sad sad bends the sky
Around the skyline, bruised, bewildered,

All our hopes projected on its scrim.
(The baby wakes. The baby speaks

Her perfect, wordless French.)
Ou sont les vandals, mon chèr,

Mon petit pois? What is
History to myth? For the vandals

Have not come—*mon serviette, mon fou*—
And the poem without them,

Like our lives alone, makes no sense.
The baby cries. The day becomes

Another day. *Ou sont les vandals,*
Mon flocon de neige, mon petit mal-de-tête?

Where are those vandals,
My porcupine, my potted fern?

THE FOUNTAIN, THE FOUNTAIN, THE VANDALS

Sing in shrill atonal harmony.
It's another poem, another way to violate

Decorum: the vandals are in
The fountain, the fountain, scooping up

The pennies. (Like God above
Scooping souls

Strewn in battle.)
Because it is a poem the vandals' glee

Rages, untempered, only words.
Across the way, leaning on a lamppost, a newly-

Retired rocket scientist
Thinks about how simple

A decent meal makes marriage seem.
The vandals shimmyshimmyshimmyshimmy shake

In the watery blpps and brbls, play
Drown-the-Kitten, Moses-in-the-Basket,

Venice-in-its-Cups.
(The scientist is unperturbed:

She suspects the vandals
Of their pieties.) And you and I?

We'd like to say that we don't notice,
Rapt as we are in our sidewalk snack—

Please pass the sugar. Another
Ginger snap?—embroiled in the imbroglio

Of life, each other, this mystery
We will not name self-interest.

The scientist bites her nail. Bite.
The Half-'n-Half becomes a metaphor.

And the vandals slosh around the square,
Proud to be the nuisance it's a vandal's

Job to be. (God cups the dead.)
And you and I drink up, look down,

Tremble, tremble, tremble.
And God spreads God's fingers,

All the dead scattered in-between
(They sink and float and soar and . . .)

AFTER THE POEM WHO KNOWS

What the vandals will do.
For now they have been sighted

At the mall, at the bank,
Down by the fire station,

At the high school make-out shack,
Everywhere that myth revises history.

I want I want I want I want!
The vandals have been heard to chant,

Their chant a chant heard far away.
(Ear to the ground, finger in the air.)

Above, a cloud,
A gull, another cloud,

Capriciousness. In the tree
At the edge of the stanza, the ghosts

Of two squirrels chase each other up
And up and up and up

Then downdowndown!
(The stanza ends.)

And you and I? Who knows
What we might do

Once the poem concludes, the vandals gone,
Our words remembered as . . .

Recidivist! screeches a screech owl.
And the vandals stomp onto

The scene, picking their teeth clean
With the chipped tips of dullèd knives.

And you and I, and you and I?
We ready ourselves for death

(O yes the poem has taught us to)
Pack up our little picnic, close the book,

And step into the future:
Hello? We're here. Is anybody home?

WAKING FROM ANOTHER DREAM, THE VANDALS

Waking from another dream, the vandals
Dream themselves awake,

Sweaty in their makeshift beds
'Neath the stars, stars, stars.

We're all awake, we're all
Sleepless in the poem together,

Curling into our bodies like
Paper burning. (Soft,

Do you smell something burning?)
Coffee pours from thermoses,

Mini-donuts pile on a plate. The vandals
Watch the stars, stars, stars

Rehearse their dying.
In the poem together, where we are

Always together, you and I
Hide behind the trees, underneath

The brambles, our little hopes
Rolled like socks into a ball.

(Mmm. Is that rosehips?
You smell nice.) The vandals lie awake,

Smoking cigarettes, the powdered
Sugar on their paper plates

Doodled in the shapes of planets,
Astrolabes, concertinas, guns.

And you and I? What of you and me?
In each other's arms we're far from

Knowing what we want.
Hah! the vandals snort.

You think you're cleverer?
And the stars, stars, stars

(Powdered sugar on a paper plate)
Go nowhere, fixed upon the sky.

VANDALS, BEES

In the poem about the vandals and the bees,
The vandals don their padded suits,

Padded gloves and padded boots,
And stroll among the hives.

(The bees are dreaming:
BZZZ they dream, which means . . .)

The vandals are out to pillage—
'Tis the season, 'tis the weekend—

They lick their chops, scrape honey
From the comb, polka

Through the wild lilies, the lilies wild
But never free (constrained by

Thermal units, annual rainfall, the occasional
Killer frost and poetry.)

Screw the greater good! the vandals shout.
And double-screw *vox populi*!

In the poem because a poem
Is wild but never free, the vandals

Remove their meshèd masks,
Glare into each other's reddened eyes,

Search for you, for me. And the bees
Dream up their ghosts: BZZZ they dream.

(The honey drips
Like minutes from the dying day.)

And the vandals flap in their protective gear,
Reel amid the wild clover,

(Yarrow, thistle, wheat, whatever.)
Look at me, they yodel. Beebeebee!

⁜

CRUELTY, THE VANDALS SAY

Is learned. In this poem they're right,
Cold and huddled 'round a trashfire

Underneath the trestle bridge,
Hunger chewing on self-pity.

Look. Here comes the boy
Who will be your father,

A glass jar in a paper bag,
Holes jammed through the metal lid

To let a doomed toad breathe.
(The boy has your hands, your smile.)

Watch him leap the ties, counting
One-oh, two-oh, three-oh, here we go.

Smell the smell: ash and creosote.
(Why must the toad die? you ask.

Because the rhyme has told us so.)
The vandals clench their frozen fingers

Into fists, sing their vandal songs
Of switching yards, railway dicks, the moon

In strips across a lover's back
(On you, on me, on the

Everlasting.) The boy unbends
A safety pin, says

Hey. C'mon. Wake up—
And skewers the toad. (Listen

For the whistle, the train
Is almost in the poem.)

And the vandals break into a howl
As the Limited roars o'er their heads

Like the very roar of Being;
And the boy hops off the tracks

—He shall not die—
Unscrews the lid, shakes out the mess

(The toad, its soul, whatever.)
Oh, you say. Oh dear, oh me oh my.

THERE IS ANOTHER YOU

Wandering the poem
Among vandals, underneath the bright

Chiffon of day. Alleyways open onto
Alleyways, fire escapes, laundered shirts

Strung like letters no one knows.
The other you is happy, maybe.

(In the back of a salon, a teenaged manicurist
Buffs her nails, left to right, 1–10.)

Beyond the poem the ack-ack of reality
Can be heard in the hills

Above the city. (There is another you
Disappearing, seen only from behind.)

Like their heroes the vandals promenade
The back streets, Disco King when

No one's watching, screwdrivers
Sharpened into shivs, sharp

As the wrath of God.
(A one-eyed tom hisses at his ghost.)

There is another you looking in a storefront
At the 54,000 poppy seeds a Korean Vet

Has collected in a plastic urn
—"One for each of us they got"—

And at the image of another you caught up
In the glass. Because a poem is like a shop window

Through which we see, in which we're caught,
What the other you might do

Becomes a symbol for . . .
And the teenaged manicurist buttons up her coat,

Hurries to her lunch—quick, the sky is darkening—
Past the vandals in their finely honed

Rapacious poses, past the tomcat
Scratching himself sore. She has to get

Good and outta here, she only has an hour,
Or she'll be replaced—"Oh, how many times

Must I tell you, Angeline?"—
By another just like you, another you.

✳

IN ABUNDANCE THE VANDALS

Runneth over, too many
Sounds for a simple song.

Calloo! Callay! O frabjous day!
The vandals shout (as though the words

Of a poem could be made louder.)
The vandals are out to catch some rays,

Their buckets full of blueberries;
Blueberries smeared across their lips,

Sloppy as a sloppy lover's kiss;
Blueberries crushed in their powerful hands;

Blueberries a profane, indecent blue
(A bear is in the poem, too.)

The vandals try to tread in single file
But stumble into 2s and 3s, trampling

The gorse, each other—they fill
Our thoughts with blueberries, enough

For you and me. (Do you feel hungry?
Hunger is what hunger needs.)

And the bear stands up.
A bear! the vandals say.

And someone else's moral code
Elbows us, nudges us into action:

You-you-you-you! we shout.
Over here, you bear!

And the poem ends in a standoff
As all poems do, everyone agog atop

The mountaintop, our lives no more
Than stylized desires. Jesus Christ!

We huff, as the last line arrives:
A bear! A real live bear!

APPEARANCES, THE VANDALS KNOW

Are always what they seem. It's another poem,
Another fall from grace, the vandals

Huddled in their scrum
Like a thought before it's thought.

Go, dogs, go! the vandals bark,
Then run to roam downtown,

Tearing out the street signs:
STOP, PED-X, DON'T WALK and WALK

Tossed into the 4 x 4, to be
Replanted randomly. On the beach,

Redundant waves. There the vandals tarry,
Arm themselves with disappointments—

SWIM AT YOUR OWN RISK and
DANGER: VOLLEYBALL.

(This time, they'll come so quietly
We might not hear them

But for the poem.) In the Hospital Zone,
The signs of indiscriminate meaning bloom

As the vandals' dirty work declares
A parking spot outside Emergency

To be THE HOME OF CELLOPHANE.
Down the street, a church proclaims

NO STANDING: MORTUARY;
At the edge of the poem a field of cows

Proffers LIVE NUDIE GIRLS.
And you and I? Caught up in our roles—

You as you, et cetera—we hold each other
Tighter, dig our heels into the comedy

As though our laughter
Could substitute

For what we can't believe.
But the vandals tire of such mindless

Ease, idling their 4 x 4
Next to you and me—Please change,

O light, please change to green—
Make pistols of their pointers,

Cock their opposable thumbs.
Bang! they say. You're history.

*

ACKNOWLEDGMENTS

The Antioch Review: "Vandals, Horses," "Vandal Sex," "Work, the Vandals Say";

The Blue Moon Review (http://www.thebluemoon.com/): "Between Poems the Vandals Go";

Boulevard: "After the Poem Who Knows," "Vandals in the Garden";

Colorado Review: "With Vengeance and Desire, the Vandals";

Columbia: "Practicing Their Diffidence, the Vandals" (as "Even Older, the Vandals"), "Vandals, Bees";

Field: "Chanson (Ou sont les Vandals?)," "Philosophy, the Vandals Say";

TriQuarterly: "Before the Vandals," "Cruelty, the Vandals Say," "The Vandals";

Washington Square: "The God of the Vandals," "The Vandals and the Law," "Without the Vandals."

"Vandals, Horses" was awarded a 1999 Pushcart Prize, and was reprinted in *The Pushcart Prize XXIII: The Best of the Small Presses*.

"Another Poem About the Vandals" is for Corinne Duchesne.

I would like to thank the following people for their insights and their support: Alice Fulton, Forrest Gander, Diana Hume George, Susan Hahn, Andrew Hudgins, Campbell McGrath, Joe Morse, Jacqueline Osherow, Lorraine Tuson, and Mark Willhardt.

ABOUT THE AUTHOR

Alan Michael Parker received his M.F.A. in Poetry from Columbia University in 1987. His poems have appeared in many magazines including *Antaeus, Boulevard, The New Republic, The New Yorker, The Paris Review,* and *TriQuarterly.* His first collection, *Days Like Prose* (Alef Books, 1997), was named a "Notable Book from 1997" by the National Book Critics Circle. His awards include fellowships from the New Jersey and Pennsylvania Councils on the Arts and a Pushcart Prize. Co-Editor of *The Routledge Anthology of Cross-Gendered Verse* (Routledge Books, 1996) and North American Editor for *Who's Who in 20th Century World Poetry* (Routledge Books, 2000), he is a regular book reviewer for *The New Yorker,* among other magazines. He teaches English and creative writing at Davidson College in North Carolina, where he lives with his wife, the painter Felicia van Bork, and their son, Eli.

BOA EDITIONS, LTD.

AMERICAN POETS CONTINUUM SERIES

Vol. 1 *The Fuhrer Bunker: A Cycle of Poems in Progress*
W. D. Snodgrass

Vol. 2 *She*
M. L. Rosenthal

Vol. 3 *Living With Distance*
Ralph J. Mills, Jr.

Vol. 4 *Not Just Any Death*
Michael Waters

Vol. 5 *That Was Then: New and Selected Poems*
Isabella Gardner

Vol. 6 *Things That Happen Where There Aren't Any People*
William Stafford

Vol. 7 *The Bridge of Change: Poems 1974–1980*
John Logan

Vol. 8 *Signatures*
Joseph Stroud

Vol. 9 *People Live Here: Selected Poems 1949–1983*
Louis Simpson

Vol. 10 *Yin*
Carolyn Kizer

Vol. 11 *Duhamel: Ideas of Order in Little Canada*
Bill Tremblay

Vol. 12 *Seeing It Was So*
Anthony Piccione

Vol. 13 *Hyam Plutzik: The Collected Poems*

Vol. 14 *Good Woman: Poems and a Memoir 1969–1980*
Lucille Clifton

Vol. 15 *Next: New Poems*
Lucille Clifton

Vol. 16 *Roxa: Voices of the Culver Family*
William B. Patrick

Vol. 17 *John Logan: The Collected Poems*

Vol. 18 *Isabella Gardner: The Collected Poems*

Vol. 19 *The Sunken Lightship*
Peter Makuck

Vol. 20 *The City in Which I Love You*
Li-Young Lee

Vol. 21 *Quilting: Poems 1987–1990*
Lucille Clifton

Vol. 22 *John Logan: The Collected Fiction*

Vol. 23 *Shenandoah and Other Verse Plays*
Delmore Schwartz

Vol. 24 *Nobody Lives on Arthur Godfrey Boulevard*
Gerald Costanzo

Vol. 25 *The Book of Names: New and Selected Poems*
Barton Sutter

Vol. 26 *Each in His Season*
W. D. Snodgrass

Vol. 27 *Wordworks: Poems Selected and New*
Richard Kostelanetz

Vol. 28 *What We Carry*
Dorianne Laux

Vol. 29 *Red Suitcase*
Naomi Shihab Nye

Vol. 30 *Song*
Brigit Pegeen Kelly

Vol. 31 *The Fuehrer Bunker: The Complete Cycle*
W. D. Snodgrass

Vol. 32 *For the Kingdom*
Anthony Piccione

Vol. 33 *The Quicken Tree*
Bill Knott

Vol. 34 *These Upraised Hands*
William B. Patrick

Vol. 35 *Crazy Horse in Stillness*
William Heyen

✳

Printed in the USA
CPSIA information can be obtained
at www.ICGtesting.com
JSHW082224140824
68134JS00015B/722